T0120869

This journey through everyday kind of experiences beckons one to quiet and deeper reflection. When Eldon writes you just want to stop an extra moment and soak in the gentle nudge of the Spirit.

Denis Keith, Executive Director of Open Hands Ministries

Eldon is a fountain of spiritual insight and gifted at listening and being fully present to those with whom he directs. He is also present to the world around him and able to quickly draw from a lifetime of listening to his experience and the voice of God through that experience. He receives others where they are and kindly and gently leads them more fully into who they were created to be. I have benefitted immensely from his voice speaking to my heart.

Conrad Kanagy

Spiritual Formation

Attention along the Way

ELDON E. FRY

This book is a work of non-fiction. Unless otherwise noted, the author and the publisher make no explicit guarantees as to the accuracy of the information contained in this book and in some cases, names of people and places have been altered to protect their privacy.

WestBow Press books may be ordered through booksellers or by contacting:

WestBow Press
A Division of Thomas Nelson & Zondervan
1663 Liberty Drive
Bloomington, IN 47403
www.westbowpress.com
844-714-3454

ISBN: 978-1-6642-2659-3 (sc)
ISBN: 978-1-6642-2661-6 (hc)
ISBN: 978-1-6642-2660-9 (e)

Library of Congress Control Number: 2021904506

Print information available on the last page.

WestBow Press rev. date: 03/29/2021

Introduction

WHAT HAPPENED ALONG YOUR LIFE JOURNEY? STUDIES OF THE brain affirm the importance of our connectors and relationship with the world outside ourself. Our experiences serve as a basis for our own formation.

Martin Laird in his book, *Into The Silent Land* says there are two contemplative practices that are essential for Christian formation. One is stillness or contemplation, the other is watchfulness or awareness. These short vignettes share how I have experienced my world and processed my perceptions, internally and externally. In the end, they became the key to my spiritual formation. I hope that as you reflect on these brief topics, you will also intentionally engage a formational process and experience transformation as you journey through your life experiences and observations of your environment.

Contents

January

A Memory

MEMORIES AT MY POINT IN LIFE CAN BRING PEALS OF LAUGHTER or tears of painful reminders. Memory is valuable for us all. There is even an app to improve memory for older folks like me.

Today was full of activity, but some of the day lent itself to remembering. I recalled the first time it began to sink into my soul that God truly loved me. That memory is etched on my soul, and I recall the time and place that awareness filled my soul with the joy of knowing God loves me. It is amazing how that experience was so different from knowledge. I knew the verses, and I had heard the testimonies, but I had not embraced God's love so freely given. Why? I am uncertain. Psychology, sociology, biology, and other disciplines have suggestions, but as much as they are pertinent and concepts cannot be discounted, the fact remains that I did not see God as loving unconditionally. Somehow, my heart had not connected with my head, even though I could recite, "I know God loves me because the Bible told me so."

Embracing God's love did not change any circumstances, but it changed me and the course of my life. Receiving unconditional love has a way of doing that. That memory—that moment that is worth more than a gold medal or any other award—is a treasure still freely given and received every day. I am loved, and it has made a difference. What a memory!

Mesmerizing

I SAT WITH THREE SPIRITUAL DIRECTORS AROUND A CRACKLING fire. At the end of our session, one person noted that the fire burning in the fireplace was "mesmerizing." Somehow, that word called for further reflection. I love campfires, especially when they provide the opportunity to share a backyard campfire with grandchildren. It is amazing that we can sit relaxed in silence and lost in thought, and at other times be caught up in animated conversation as the shadows created by the firelight flicker around us.

What is it about the fire in a fireplace that catches and holds our attention? The flicker reminds me of the tenuousness of life. I am compelled to hold my breath, hoping the fire will continue to burn. It may have to do with the dance and the variety of flames as they rise toward the chimney or images created by the flames and the sense of excitement and anticipation of what will be shaped next by the fire. Few things in life seem capable of holding my attention for such a length of time. Truly, the logs succumbing to the fire are mesmerizing. Somehow, the invitation to gather around a fireplace to enjoy the fire reminds me in this Epiphany season of the invitation to worship God, "for our God is a consuming fire" (Hebrews 12:29 NIV). God with us is mesmerizing.

Dr. Martin Luther King Jr.

We are on the eve of the Dr. Martin Luther King Jr. holiday. Dr. King responded to the "I must" of life. I recognize that Dr. King did not respond to God's call so that we would honor his memory with a national holiday. He simply responded to what he discerned God was saying in the reality of his world. He was willing to address injustice on multiple levels and make a difference that we continue to embrace today. The idea that we would recognize this as a day of remembrance and recommitment to his purposes by being involved in service to others perhaps summarizes the beat of his heart. He was willing to sacrifice personal goals and dreams to serve our nation.

That challenge is personalized when I ask myself, "What am I doing for others?" As I celebrate this holiday, I must face that question. Jesus also challenges me by stating, "Whatever you do for the least of these … you did for me" (Matthew 24:12). Tonight, I sit with that challenge and am grateful for those who have gone before me and challenged to serve others tomorrow.

Play

I WAS INVITED TO AN EVENT PLANNED AND PRODUCED BY Short Notice Theater. It was fun because it involved grandchildren, creativity, and a play with a purpose. But it caused me to think about the number of occurrences in my life that have been initiated on short notice.

There is something about Short Notice that is both exhilarating and ominous. I desire to be spontaneous and love creativity more than repetition, yet short notice can also be unexpected pressure to make a quick decision with long-term consequences.

As I sat with someone early this morning in prayerful conversation, we reflected on how he made a short-notice decision that definitely will affect his life for some time. The decision seemed sudden and even mystical, yet the truth is that he has faithfully prepared himself to experience God at work within, even in times of great silence. Those disciplines prepared him to respond on short notice.

When we have prepared ourselves for years, that unexpected moment of crisis or insight is not a child of the moment as much as readiness for the appropriate response. I found myself desiring to be more faithful in my own practices to respond to the invitation to Short Notice Theater in my life.

Surprise

HAVE YOU EVER PURCHASED A SURPRISE FOR SOMEONE THAT you just could not wait to share with him or her? Today, I happened on an opportunity that I knew was just the right gift. If you knew me well, you would know that my strength is not gift giving. I struggle at Christmas and birthdays to select the right gift. I always second-guess if the one I chose will be meaningful for the recipient. Maybe I am the only one who experiences that conflicted tension, but at least for me, it is very real. My discovery of an appropriate gift certainly raised a new level of excitement in me.

In these early days of Epiphany, where we celebrate the gift of Christ in our lives, I wonder how God, the giver of the exceptional gift of Jesus to humanity, must have felt. I realize that ascribing human feelings to God is a theological nightmare. But I still wonder if God felt the excitement of knowing Christ among us was the best gift ever. Was that why a "heavenly host" would celebrate in the hillsides around Bethlehem? The carol expresses the annunciation of the angel to Mary as "glad tidings." Is that a reflection of the anticipation God experienced? I will not know the answer to that question in my lifetime, but finding the right gift surely brings a big smile and deep satisfaction.

Wind

THE WIND IS BLOWING TONIGHT, FORCING THE TEMPERATURE to feel like the wind chill is below zero. Even the whistle of the passing train seems frozen in the air. Whew. Watching the swaying of leafless trees and listening to the currents of arctic air whistling around the corners of our cabin reminds me of watching *The Long Hard Winter* in South Dakota, except the wind was from a giant fan and the snow machine only pretended it was working. But the cold and the wail of the wind tonight are real.

The wind reminds me of days in Israel and the words of Christ that seemed to be in the air. "The wind blows wherever it pleases. You hear its sound, but you cannot tell where it comes from or where it is going. So is everyone who is born of the Spirit" (John 3:8 NIV). Today, I spent time with some people involved in ministry. All of us are in second careers and trying to follow God into a new season of life. Our stories were encouraging but surprising. None of us would have guessed our current vocations, but somehow, God seems to be blowing the wind of the Spirit on our lives, and we are trying to understand where it is taking us. As we shook hands, prayed, and parted, we all felt the urgency of the wind blowing.

February

Anticipation

I WAS SURPRISED AT HOW BUSY THE GROCERY STORE WAS WHEN I was doing our weekly shopping. I remembered that the weather forecast called for a major snowstorm tonight. People were scurrying down the aisles, racing against time to get stocked up to survive the oncoming snow. Rudeness, both intentional and unintentional, in the rush seemed to invade the usually laid-back folks who shop midafternoon. Even the parking lot appeared to be a place of hurrying home or to other errands because of the imminent threat of snow. Not a single flake had fallen. Nor had it yet five hours later. The anticipation of threat created an increased tension, resulting in a flurry of activity within us.

The anticipation of a change in weather changed us, including me. I wonder how many times I have allowed my life to become frenzied because of the threats I anticipate. I hope I will react with calm in the anticipation and even the reality of storms in life. I spoke today with a person who has intentionally resisted being pressured by anticipated storms and instead has embraced the calm of listening. Storms will come, but I live with the awareness that I can act with "the peace that passes all understanding" (Philippians 4:7). There is still a storm in the forecast, but I am at peace.

Ash Wednesday

"Remember you are dust, and to dust you shall return" is spoken as the sign of the cross is inscribed on our foreheads, reminding us of our Lenten journey with Christ to the cross. Ash Wednesday is a day of fasting and prayer. My day has been full of prayer with a variety of people. As I traveled to our designated meeting places, I noticed that because of recent snow and treatment on the highways, virtually all vehicles were covered in dust. The dusty vehicles were carrying people going somewhere with the intent to do something. Each passing vehicle reminded me of my own temporariness.

Later, I noticed that there was a grouping of vehicles that had no dust-covered frames. Those vehicles were parked in sales lots. They were not traveling anywhere, which seems like a reflection of life. It is a dusty and very human journey we are on. Only those remaining still avoid the dust of life. Those on the journey encounter the dirt of the road.

Kneeling at an altar receiving the institution of the ashes and hearing familiar words reminds me that I am joining Christ on a purposeful journey. I am reminded that the dust is symbolic of my humanity, while at the same time, it reminds me of the holy journey we call Lent that is ahead.

Beauty

The beautiful snow cover is receding in our woods, revealing the broken limbs and mesh of fallen leaves. I am enticed to begin spring cleanup. I actually hope that the Groundhog Day forecast is accurate and spring is just around the corner of time. In the meantime, I throw the broken limbs in the driveway out into the trees, knowing I will need to pick them up again. I find myself pondering how I will go about cleanup and prioritizing steps to accomplish this good work.

Like the receding snow, life changes the landscape of my life as I watch with disbelieving eyes. What once was the scenic beauty of layered snow is losing its masquerading cover-up, revealing the broken, wind-tossed, and less desirable qualities of human life. Energetic hopefulness seems determined to melt away, leaving a drabber and less inviting reality. But even as I gaze on this melting loss, I realize that a new and different beauty is arising from the stillness of snow cover. The mix of shapes and colors paints a new form of beauty. I find myself enjoying the masterpiece and thanking the God of all seasons that my life does not remain covered in the facade of sameness.

Ode to a Valentine

What saintly kiss this ruse began,
This playful holiness.
We celebrate with gifts of love,
Embracing cupid's messiness.

Loneliness is lost in love
Or maybe just resettled
To spaces yet unsurveyed,
Where cynics have not meddled.

So we wink and hug each other,
Exchanging cards to a lover
Words of love, shared desire,
Setting longing hearts afire.

So, this Valentine's Day of giving
Holy love, we remember,
Knowing God created living
And gave us one another.

Contrasts

Contrasts can be beautiful. As they appear side by side, each highlights the beauty of the other. I noticed that this evening as the crimson sunset streaked across the lightly clouded sky, creating hues of red that glowed in contrast to the white snow-covered fields. The beauty of each was stunning, but the contrast enhanced the beauty.

In life, there are so many contrasts in our multiple differences (some obvious others more hidden). But rather than diminish each other, our differences are really opportunities to highlight and enhance each other in our significant differences. It almost sounds "hokey" as I think about how simple the idea is, but I see it in so many places and from different vantage points.

Contrasts are beautiful, but I must confess, too often I do not appreciate what has formed these differences. In the case of central Pennsylvania, it is too much snow (my opinion). I am snow weary. But if we had not had the snow, it would not have contrasted so beautifully with the sunset. Sometimes it is easier to gripe about the differences than to appreciate them.

Sadly, in the journey of Christ that we honor in this Lenten season, there were people who could not appreciate or even tolerate differences. That rejection took its toll on many lives, both at the time and continuing now even centuries later. If I refuse to allow contrasts, the sameness of all things will mute the beauty of possibilities. Life will be bland. So tonight, I pause to give thanks for the differences I experience and pray that I may never become crotchety in my aging process, refusing to enjoy the contrasts.

Waiting

TODAY, WE WAITED ON THE DELIVERY OF AN ESSENTIAL PIECE of equipment to finish a project. Much of our life is filled with waiting. I used to say things like, "I can't wait to grow up." But of course, we have to wait. We cannot simply will ourselves to grow up and see it suddenly happen like the beanstalk in the delightful children's story. Some sermons I heard seemed to promise the idea that all things would change instantly "if only I would (you can fill in the blank)." God seems to work in the instantaneous at times, but the story often is elongated by waiting. For Jesus, there is thirty-three years of waiting to fulfill his purpose. He experienced the instantaneous in marvelous stories, but he also spent long years of anticipating the culmination of his life's work here among us.

Waiting is never a comfortable process for me. It feels awkward, and sometimes, it feels unexplainable, even irresponsible. Yet, God moves in these mysterious ways with a very different timetable or way of accounting time than I do. I resonate with the frustrated Martha (John 11), confronting Jesus with, "If you had been here, my brother would not have died" (:21). I have murmured in my waiting, "If only …" too many times to count. Yet, God has moved forward at an inexorably slow pace. But often, I can review the slow pace and see that God accomplished a monumental purpose.

Lent is a turtle pace in a rabbit world. We hear over and over that our world is speeding up. Like a merry-go-round, it seems to pick up speed until the only thing left is to hold on and beg for it to slow down so we can survive. Lent is a gift of slowing down and waiting. Instead of looking at the world through dizzying speed, I can begin to see more clearly and become aware that God is nearer than I thought in my spinning cycle. Thank God for this space we name Lent began hundreds of years ago by followers of Christ, who knew I would need this time to put life on pause and wait with the multitudes of believers to celebrate a resurrection that gives me hope to face life in this speeding life. Tonight, I can value waiting, but I know tomorrow impatience will knock at the door.

March

Fog

THIS MORNING A HEAVY FOG INVADED THE WOODS AROUND our cabin until the trees looked like some scene from a horror movie. I felt I needed to ask myself if it was safe to go outside. Not only did the fog bring a different look to our woods, but the air smelled different, and the view between the barren trees was limited to a few yards beyond our driveway. The fog persisted until nearly noon. Finally, the rain formed in the fog arrived. The cold, wet drops made me glad my business was indoors today.

As I think about the fog this evening, I realize that the journey of my life at times is surrounded by a besetting fogginess that changes the landscape and creates a certain concern of what may be hidden in the folds of the grayish darkness. Fogginess obstructs my view and prevents the clarity I value. I have been lost in the fog of self-absorbed desires and selfishly motivated actions. Because Christ modeled a willingness to break through the fog of our world by choosing to empty himself to the lowliness of a manger only to exalted "to the highest place and gave him the name that is above every name" (Philippians 2:6–11). Advent is a pilgrimage to the place where the fog of my darkness is rolled back and I can see with clarity.

I Love Cool

I LOVE COOL. COOL DAYS LIKE TODAY. ALLERGIES ARE MINIMAL, and the air is clear, so visibility is in miles, not feet, and energy levels are up because sweat is limited while working. It was cool today, and I have enjoyed it!

I realize that my friends who like fun in the sun grit their teeth on cool days because the heat level is low.

Preferences differ and often are individualized or even community oriented in things such as the athletic team I support. Preferences vary, and yet, they need to be differentiated from principles in terms of making decisions. The type of salad dressing I enjoy is a preference.

When I confuse preference with principle, I create unnecessary separation from others. Tolerance is not a bad word in the world of preferences. I tolerate people who cheer against my team, but that difference should not separate us. That would only happen if someone turned that preference into a principle. Someone who does that, for instance, might not let anyone in their house who did not cheer for their team.

It is sad on many levels but particularly sad when it comes to faith issues. Why would I let my preferences keep me from loving a brother or sister with different preferences? That would be tragic.

Tonight, I pray that we will allow for differing preferences and embrace common principles that allow us to fulfill Christ's prayer that we impress the world by how we love each other. Allowing for preferences is a beginning. I realize it is not always easy to differentiate from principles. But as a Christ follower, we must!

Melting

THE BEAUTY OF THE DEEP SNOW COVER IS MELTING RAPIDLY under the warmth of an early spring thaw. Eaves are dripping rapidly, and nearby streams are nearing overflow. The snow was beautiful as it covered the landscape and insulated whatever it covered from the bitter cold that followed. It felt as if we had taken up residence in an oversized freezer. Everything was cold and frozen and radiated only zero-degree potential.

As the sunset directs its multihued beams toward the earth and nature begins to turn off the lights of the brilliant day, the sheen that mirrors off the frozen snow cover has changed. As I look out into our woods and shrinking snow cover, I realize that the frozen layers have softened and even melted away during this pleasant day. I can visualize the warmth from the window view tonight. The melting of a frozen heart can bring warmth to hearts locked in the icebox of circumstances and create hope for a spring of new possibilities. As I look out the window, I sense that the warm light on the cold of my soul can melt the frozen blocks of resistance to the life of the Son this Lenten season.

Tonight

Tonight, our dog is sitting between my legs. She is a brave hearted dog, but thunder is worrisome to her. Somehow she feels safer between my legs with her head resting on my foot. She is determined to stay there.

Unfortunately, our dog reminds me of myself. I run to God with my bravado missing at the first crack of storms in my life and want God's reassuring presence to remind me it will be OK. It was in the midst of a severe Idaho mountain storm that my mother taught me Isaiah 41:10. I learned those words while standing on an open porch, facing lightning striking around us and thunder roaring loudly. They still have a calming effect on my soul. "Fear not, for I am with you; be not dismayed for I am your God. I will strengthen you and help you and uphold you with the righteousness of my right hand." I know storms are not the context of that passage, but it has served as a reminder that God is present in the storms of my life. I gather a sense of protection and confidence; I suppose much like my dog does laying between my legs.

As the sun begins to break through and the powerful display of nature has turned to quiet, my soul reflects on the storms of life that have brought me to my knees, seeking God's protection and help. One of God's self-descriptive names is translated, "God the protector." It does not mean bad things cannot happen, but that reassurance does strengthen my confidence. Little wonder that the messengers of God said so many times to their recipients, “Fear not!” Somehow that is enough even tonight.

Underground Railroad

I SPENT SEVERAL HOURS IN RETREAT WITH SOME VERY SPECIAL pastors of an urban church that is intentionally multicultural and committed to diversity. The place where we met was a stopover site for the Underground Railroad. As the co-owner showed us the secret flooring that opened to the darkness underneath the "cookhouse," I watched these pastors connect to far more than a history lesson because their hearts are committed to racial reconciliation. They virtually live and breathe that commitment. When the flooring was removed and they peered for the first time into the underground space, history became tangible.

As they individually let themselves down into the darkened space, it was easy to imagine someone following the trails along the Susquehanna River and walking carefully through the shadows of the fields to this house on the edge of frontier, hoping it was true that a safe space awaited them. There were neighbors that did not approve and would have quickly turned them in for the reward offered.

I saw tears, hugs, and jaws set, determined to stay the course of racial reconciliation as their imaginations touched reality. I was humbled and honored to be an observer. Somewhere deep inside me, I experienced a renewed love for my pastors and felt honored to be with people committed to the ministry of reconciliation (2 Corinthians 5:18–19).

Weight

Decision made. The weight of the decision is gone, and breathing becomes easier. Sometimes, I wonder if I have a daily quota for decisions and if I cross over the limit, they transform from decisions to burdens. In the process of becoming burdens, they gain weight—enough to crush the soul. I lived joyfully until faced with a certain decision, and then it seemed as if I had just attempted to lift an elephant.

Decision-making reflects my control. The potential for mistakes is obvious, and the weight of ownership drives home the reality that this is my responsibility. No wonder Jesus gave an invitation to take His yoke upon us while indicating that His yoke is easy and burden light. Having Christ share the load lightens the weight of decision-making. In my mind, Christ entering the process changes the pressure of decision-making to an experience of joint discernment. It is like pressing the release valve of a pressure cooker. In a matter of seconds, the pressure building for hours is freed.

Tonight, a decision made was transformed through a communal process of discernment. While it remains a mystery how Christ is present in these decisions, looking back, there is no doubt that His presence was very real and His guidance was discerned and affirmed by us all. I can sleep tonight free of the weight a pressured decision attempted to pile on me. I thank God for those who traveled the rough road through the discerning process, and I can honestly leave the results to God. Sweet rest.

April

Focus

She almost ran over me! I saw this car in my review mirror, rapidly gaining on me. It was a country road with no place to pull out of her way. Fortunately, she looked up and slowed down as I sped up. Whew! As we drove on, I realized she was doing her makeup as she drove. She was distracted and speeding. Most of us have stories about a close call, when either we or someone else was driving distracted.

Now, a few days later, I can reflect on that incident without my blood pressure rising. As I think about it, it seems our culture is not only dealing with the eight deadly sins identified by early Christians. I have presumptuously added a ninth, "distraction." My life is bombarded by multiple forms of technology and multiplied activities to complete in the fast-paced culture we live in today. The spiritual impact on me really is as devastating as distracted driving. Too many times, the distractions of my life have taken my attention off of God. The sounds of technology that I embrace seem to eliminate the quiet listening I need to find my way in the spiritual maze of my world. I need to prioritize like the example held in this text: "This one thing I do ..." (Philippians 3:13 NIV).

The use of technology is not the issue. Rather, the restlessness in my soul is not satisfied by technology but longs for the silence that allows me to listen to the sounds of God speaking. To hear

God's voice, I need to focus on listening. Like Samuel, I need to assert, "Speak, for your servant is listening" (1 Samuel 3:10). So, for a few minutes tonight, I plan to drive life's highway undistracted, focused on one thing. I will benefit from what I hear and learn there.

Helping Me

Have you ever intended to help someone else and realized in the process that God actually intended it to help you? Someone talked to me during spiritual direction of a wonderful plan to engage people he loves in a Sabbath experience. It was a worthy vision and connected to his passion and training. But as he described the many barriers his plan faced and the challenges of accomplishing his worthy goal, I found myself asking whether he thought that maybe God was inviting him to experience Sabbath. After a long pause and reflective thought, he was surprised to realize that maybe this effort was really God's invitation for him to experience the Sabbath. He affirmed his need for Sabbath to allow his soul to heal.

Although I have no research to assert how often this is the case, it has been my own experience and observation that our deep intentions are often motivated by our own hidden needs. Sometimes others need the care, but the story may really be about us. Jesus told an engaging story of a Jewish man beaten and left for dead along the treacherous Jericho road. Fortunately, a Samaritan, who was a despised and marginalized man, stopped to help and carried him to Jericho. Who was God helping? Was it the beaten man or the marginalized man? Perhaps it was both. I do not know, except I am convinced that sometimes I have benefited more from the caretaking than the roadside victim. Serving Jesus seems to turn some things in my world upside down and inside out. I am finding I need to be attentive to the meaning of the event. God speaks in mysterious ways.

Muddling

I WAS IN A PLACE OF BUSINESS WHERE A LOT SEEMED TO BE going wrong, and one clerk stated emphatically, "I should just have stayed in bed today." I have had days like that, where everything I was involved in seemed out of sync. Later, I spoke with a person who said they had a wonderful "quiet time." Then, within the hour, *boom!*, all tranquility seemed to be lost in multiple crises. I have found there are many days in my life when I do what I call "muddling through." There are days when I begin with a sense of purpose but lose perspective as a variety of factors collide to create confusion, even chaos.

I can only imagine what the initial days were like as Mary and Joseph waited on the pregnancy. I assume after a visit from Gabriel, everything else seemed very mundane and even confusing enough that each day seemed like muddling through. Then there were those awful taxes. I am so grateful that they were people of character willing to muddle through the daily to deliver the Savior. As I reflect on Advent, I find myself muddling through the hype, the pressure, the decisions, and even the disappointments, but I believe an important part of the spiritual journey is muddling through.

Selma

RECENTLY, I SPENT TIME WITH A PERSON WHO MARCHED IN Selma. He spoke of how as a college student in Nebraska, he was moved by the sight of children being beaten. Something inside him said, "You must let them know someone outside of their community cares about what is happening in their world." He risked failing classes and misunderstanding by peers to initiate going to Selma, but he did not see himself as heroic. Rather, as he told his story, he marveled at the hospitality he and others experienced as they came to Selma. Something strongly spiritual was reflected from the fire of his passion. Together, we explored the spiritual implications of his time in Selma and subsequent return to campus.

In *Leadership Prayers* by Richard Krigbaum, he prays, "If you [God] will whisper the cues, I will improvise." As I listened to my friend's story of Selma, I prayed silently, "Oh, God, please forgive me for not listening to 'the cues.' I want to listen now." The noise of the daily seems to drown out the cues spoken into my life by God. God is there, and God is not silent. My friend reminded me to listen to the cues. When I hear the cues, God smiles while I improvise. But I need to be alert to catch the cues. In the silence, I can listen.

Sabbath

This week someone asked me how to discern God's leadership in the process of decision-making. They understood it was not necessarily a simple process but genuinely wanted to understand how God might lead them to discern God's direction as they made some difficult decisions. Jesus made it clear that in seeking, we would find. Somehow, in the process of openness of hands that hold preferences loosely, and with willing hearts, trusting God is speaking out of love for us, we can begin to reflect on where and how we know God is at work. It is in our willingness to humble ourselves before the Lord and others so that God can speak deeply into our lives individually and as a community. There is pressure in our world simply to make decisions quickly because time is money and because we live our culture at intense speeds. But when we take time for a sacred pause to allow God to enter our decision-making process, I have found that the decisions I make through the discernment process are often very different from those I make if pushed for an immediate decision. There are many ancient methods used by people of faith toward discernment, but they have common themes that begin with humble reflection. As I sit here on Sabbath eve, I take a sacred pause to reflect while holding possibilities loosely. I am privileged to have dear friends who are committed to prayerful reflection even though they are not directly asked to do so. Tonight began my Sabbath, and I invite those of you who read this post to prayerfully join with me as we pause together this Sabbath.

Snipes

Growing up in the Bitterroot Mountains meant I needed creative activities for entertainment. One that we enjoyed on many occasions was snipe hunting. It involved setting up a "greenhorn" with tall tales of catching snipes. Snipes are mythical nocturnal creatures that one can supposedly catch by sitting next to a trail in the forest and waiting until they come down the path and then leaping on them with a sack. We would take the greenhorn out into the forest then scatter. Instead of hunting, we would come back to our beds and wait for the greenhorn to wise up and come stumbling in during early morning hours. Of course, it was great fun for the perpetrators, probably not as much fun for the greenhorn.

Sometimes, life seems like a mythical beast I am chasing after. When the last rays of the day disappear into darkness, I find myself trying to understand how to catch life. There are so many promises, but like snipe hunting, they always seem to leave my sack empty. I return back to another day, chagrined at my ignorance. Jesus made it clear that I do not have to hunt life in the dark but that He came to bring "life and that more abundantly" (John 10:10 NIV). Thankfully, He never leaves me in the darkness but is himself the Light.

May

A Seasoned Tree

THE TREE MADE A BOLD STATEMENT IN THE FOGGY MIST OF A dreary day. As I sat in the comfort of a friendly chair and enjoyed conversation with dear friends, my gaze fell on the stately monarch. Its gnarled and knotty branches, twisted by years of changing weather and multiple seasons, reached out across the well-kept yard, a virtual feeding ground for the deer edging out of the darkening forest. Moss-covered limbs attested to years of faithful summer shade and resistance against the whirling winds and loss of leaves each autumn.

As it does to that seasoned tree, life takes its best shots at each of us. Yet, as we survive the ferocity of the changes in our lives, there comes a stateliness that is a witness to the faithfulness of God through the challenges we call living. I felt like praying for that tree to stand tall and survive the changes around and in us. These bodies seem to lose their strength, allowing drooped backs and hunched shoulders to announce the aging process, but the tree encouraged me to stand tall and not give in quickly, because my resistance develops strength. Please, aged tree, stand as a silent reminder to me that although moss may gather and cover the beauty of youth, there is still purpose in these senior years.

Birds

I TRUDGED THROUGH THE SNOW PILED DEEP OUTSIDE OUR house to check the birdfeeder. The number of birds settling for the seeds lying in the snow rather than landing on the birdfeeder indicated their food was in low supply. I was concerned for the birds because it was cold and snowy, and feed in the trees was minimal now. So, I left the warmth of our living room and entered the frozen scape behind our house. My presence scared the birds away for a time, but they would return. It was a cold journey; however, it was one I was glad to make.

As I sit here tonight reflecting on my day, I think of the words of Jesus: "Consider the ravens: They do not sow or reap, they have no storeroom or barn; yet God feeds them. And how much more valuable you are than birds!" (Luke 12:24 NIV). What motivated me to go back out into the freezing cold again today? It was simple: I cared about the birds. What moves God is also simple. God cares about us. But I noticed something else. Sometimes, we are privileged to be the one God allows to make a difference in something or someone's life. Despite the cold, I felt a warmth inside for having cared for the birds.

Chipmunk

Ode to Courage

Lowly munk, zenith of courage,
Braving odds for winter storage,
Valor marks your quick twitching,
Foraging for fun, maybe just pitching,
A huckster's story, to keep us smiling
Amazing gifts to recall the filing.
Filled with inner joy as you scatter,
Causing noise and constant chatter.
But even deeper is my respect.
You are the hero as I reflect,
Engaged so fully in daily work,
Ordinary role you refuse to shirk.
Little munk, you teach me well,
Living joyfully, I can tell,
Treasured efforts made so bravely,
Ordinary work practiced daily.
Honor with a medal? Would you care?
No, there you sit with silly stare.

Enjoy your day and respect the chipmunks.

Life Story

TODAY, OVER LUNCH, I LISTENED TO AN UNIMAGINABLE STORY shared by a young international student. He seemed too young to have engaged in all the challenges he has faced and to have experienced all the movements of God he has experienced. His family has experienced great difficulties, which still creates enigmas for this young person. Yet he persists! Miracles and pain seemed to flow from every aspect of his story. He has not always made the best choices or even honored himself or trusted God, but through it all, he continued learning and growing. It was a privilege to break bread with someone who had been on such a journey. I am humbled. It was a privilege to sit with him and listen.

Sometimes people shake their heads and wonder about this generation, but I have to say that I have been privileged to come alongside these students. We met for the first time only minutes before sharing lunch, yet he openly revealed the stories of his short life. He was not afraid to express the intensity of his reality. He was kind as he listened to my few words and interpreted them into his life story. His story deeply moves me to believe in this generation and hope that the gospel of Jesus Christ will impact our future despite overwhelming odds. How can one get up off the canvas of life and reengage the battles of life, believing that the lessons from his failures and his accomplishments combine in a vision of God working through him? How can I not love such young people? I cannot ignore such faith and willingness to engage today's challenges. Tonight, I can rest in the thought that the future of the Kingdom of God is in the good hands of these young people. I pray for them and thank God for the privilege of such conversations.

My Desire

I HAVE BEEN SITTING HERE WITH WHAT FEELS LIKE A BIG question: What is my real desire? When I pray, "Thy will be done," is that authentic, or does it mean I am glad for God's will to be done as long as it fits in the parameters of my will? I want to avoid being overly introspective, yet I feel this is a question that begs an answer.

It is probably true that as much as I would like to think I am being totally honest when I pray, "Thy will be done," I realize that, too often, I want to shape what I think is God's will rather than trusting God to work out and reveal the purpose of His will. It is not that I am antagonistic toward God's will. In reality, my will desires to engage God's will, but my will is developed by a finite individual who is not God. (That is not news!) Therefore, my will is not comprehensive like God's will but because it begins within me, I am tempted to prioritize my will. My will has often been birthed in my own desires before attempting to know God's purposes.

The good news about this process I call spiritual formation is that God allows me the time and process to learn more about who He is so I can mold my own will to be influenced by how I continue to understand Him. Therefore, I can better align with His will. It is a challenge because some days, I do better at engaging the scope of God's perspective than others. But the desire for God's will to be done exists deep within my soul, so I keep following and learning and hoping that somehow I am becoming a better reflection of God's will. So, tonight, I think I embrace as much as I know: "Thy will be done." I rest in that as true but allow for growth.

Peeking

A NEW ADDITION WAS BIRTHED AT OUR CABIN THIS WEEK. IT peeked its head over the top of the nest for the first time. For days, we have not opened our blinds for fear that the eggs would not hatch if we scared mama robin off the nest. But despite marauding blue jays and the nest being so close to our always-used screen door, the baby bird broke through its shell and has kept busy reminding its parents that it is hungry. Welcome to your world, baby robin. It is a challenging world with swooping hawks and squirrels that empty birdfeeders and an occasional cat needing lunch as it traverses the neighborhood. But despite the odds, you made it.

The cycles of life present new challenges. Some look pretty scary when we peek over the edges to gauge what kind of world we are living in. As intimidating as the changes appear, if the bird grows stronger and learns to fly, a whole new world of experiences will be available. I need to watch and learn from the life of a robin as I experience unexpected transitions. The prophet Isaiah declared, "Those who hope in the Lord … will soar on wings like eagles." I just need to learn to fly!

June

Caring

I WATCHED WITH AMUSEMENT AS A TINY HUMMINGBIRD flitted from flower to flower to gain nectar to energize its hyperactive wings. As I enjoyed the sight, I realized the flowers were drooping a bit because they were under an eave and had missed the benefit of recent rains. I also saw another flower leaning from the flower box above the door. I filled a bucket with water and drenched the drooping flowers, which were brilliant and upright this night. The leaning flower just required me to reset it in the foam of the flower box because it was made of plastic. That action reminded me of relationships in my life.

I wondered how many times I had acted with good intentions, watering the plastic flowers of life or attempting to push the real flowers into place. I am sure I have made assumptions that have created more harm than help to people I cared about. While good intentions are a beginning point, understanding real needs and responding appropriately is important in relationships.

Today, I sat with a wonderful person who was processing his care for his children. There were tears and layers of stories that reflected a prayerful caring and new insights into his role with people he loves deeply. As I drove home today, I reflected on my own life, both the good moments and the mistakes. I prayed for those I may have hurt even with my good intentions and gratefully praised the God who knows our circumstances and even our "inner most being" (Psalm 139:13) and cares appropriately.

Choices

HE MADE A WRONG CHOICE RESULTING IN A *CRACK*! IT WAS unavoidable but gut-wrenching. Two squirrels, for some unknown reason, were in the center of a narrow road. I attempted to slow down. One scampered safely off to one side, but for some mysterious reason, the second squirrel changed directions and ran under my truck wheels, resulting in a sickening sound that identified his demise. He never moved from that place. Although squirrels can be pests, this was not my desired outcome.

Recently, I have confronted some "squirrely" choices (to use the Idaho vernacular). Indecision is dangerous on the road of life, and it is easy to get fatally squished. Fortunately, God has provided protection in my less-than-excellent moments. Jesus knew Himself and His Father's will so well that one translation notes that he set his face "like flint" toward Jerusalem. He was consistently purposeful during the surrounding pressures of this Holy Week. While others played the games in the quicksand environs, he resisted the urge to choose the path of least resistance. He made a choice and followed his Father's heart. Choices matter, and I pray that I too make holy choices in a swirling world of shifting values.

Fragrance

CAN I REALLY SMELL THE FRAGRANCE OF GOD? A contemporary song by Matt Maher has this refrain: "Your fragrance is intoxicating in a secret place." Most people refer to "feeling" or "experiencing" God. I have not heard someone say, "I smelled the presence of the Lord" when they have stepped aside to meet with God. So much of our manufactured works is sickeningly sweet, what some call cheap perfume. What is the penetrating wisp of perfume that speaks of God's presence? Is it in the conversation I just had with a colleague that was "sweet" and sacred? Is it that time when, like the hymn, we sing of a "sweet, sweet presence in this place"?

I find myself cautious as I ask these questions because many merchandizers claim they have the "secret" formula of God's but and it turns out to be a knockoff at best and totally counterfeit at worst. Despite repeated warnings of scams, there is something deep inside that longs for the lasting fragrance of the holy. So, despite unscrupulous salesmen and a history of betrayal, our inner yearning persists.

When the cheap is so readily available, who would have blamed Mary for substituting for the costly "spikenard" to anoint the feet of Jesus? Her generous gift is the very fragrance of worship that Jesus carries into the room. In those simple acts of humility, in secret places, there can be awareness that God is present by the sweetness that one can smell. I have experienced that fragrance today, and I know it is the presence of the Lord.

Leftovers

I HAVE ALWAYS ENJOYED LEFTOVERS. SOMETIMES THEY REMAIN tasty and may even surpass the original meal. That is a pleasant surprise. But as I think of leftovers tonight, I am thinking about some of the people who have received my leftovers. Occasionally, it involved food, but more often, it involved clothes, furniture, and change. As I reflect on the people who have gratefully received my leftovers, I find my thoughts expanding and prayerfully considering so many in our world who are living one step from desperation yet are willing to gratefully receive crumbs from the table of my life. That thought weighs heavily in my heart.

I am watching people from Uganda who have done so much with our leftovers to educate people caught in the bloody political struggles. The same is true in Rwanda and other war-torn countries. I am also thinking of a local Haitian family that will feel like their tiny apartment is finally home as they receive our used furniture. I am also visualizing the clothes that I discard to Community Aid or the Salvation Army, and I realize all that is good and should not be discouraged. But somehow, my heart is broken, knowing that so many live on the subsistence of this world while I enjoy bounty and options.

As I reflect on the weight of this, I am also enamored by the character of people who find joy in leftovers and do not demand more or complain that God is unfair. I am keenly aware of my own complaints I have offered before God even today. My concerns are important to me, but so much of my life is focused on trivial concerns, with little impact on the ministry God has called me to serve.

I am not morbid or self-flagellating, but it is important to reflect on my priorities and consider whether I am only capable of offering leftovers or whether I share from the table of my life before my meal becomes leftovers. I am certain that even my own family has struggled at times to receive from my table. As I quiet my soul tonight, I confess that I have not always shared freely from my life table, but there have been times when generosity has won over selfishness. Those are good moments to celebrate even as I reflect on leftovers.

Mirror

One of the surprises of growing older is what I see in the mirror. I always expect to see someone about forty years old, but that is not what the mirror reflects. It is fine with me to joke about all the surprises I see in the mirror, especially in the mornings, but mirrors are important tools that reflect what is real.

Today, I am spending time working on leading a clearness committee for a good friend as he considers his future vocation. One of the striking qualifications for people who sit on a clearness committee is that they be excellent "mirrors" of what they are hearing and discerning as they meet.

I see the value of such friends. Too often, I miss reality and important decisions if I do not have real "mirrors" that reflect the truth back to me. Jesus was clear that the truth (even when not appreciated) makes us free (John 8:32). Stumbling through life in the fuzziness of poor reflections means that some important aspects of myself are never understood or addressed. Little wonder that the wise man declares, "Wounds from a friend can be trusted" (Proverbs 27:6). Mirrors that reflect truthfully are a gift. I am reflecting on the kind of mirror I need but also on whether I am a worthy mirror for my friends. I know that I need a mirror that provides a true reflection of myself, and I desire to be that kind of friend to people I care about. It is a worthy reflection.

Next Step

A recent remark by someone made me pause and reflect on the difference between "next steps" and "the next step." Planning my next steps tends to involve looking out into the future and making assumptions about what I might do in that space, while the next step is close at hand and is simply focused on the necessary immediate.

I have spent too much time focused on what might be and how I might approach it. It feels a bit like the proverbial donkey and carrot. If I plan it, it will motivate me to keep going. I am not against planning for the future; in fact, I believe it is necessary. But I have found that focusing only on my future can consume my life preventing me from being present in the now. In fact, that has happened with too much regularity in my life. I have lived for "someday" and not lived enough in today. I realize it requires some degree of balance. Perhaps this is the place to confess that I have been unbalanced too often.

By taking the next necessary next step, I am more likely to be attentive to what is around me. When I am more aware of the present, I increase the possibility of experiencing an awareness of God's presence. Worry tends to be sourced in concerns for the future, while confidence comes more easily when I am focused on the next step. Frankly, my sense is that God is coaching me to take the next step. If I am obedient and move forward, I make it easier for God to guide me. Some of my long-range plans tend to lock me into my way, leaving me with less ability adjust to God speaking into my life.

So, tonight, as I ponder this transitional time in my life. I am aware that it is not my thirty-year plan of appropriate steps that will help me arrive as a successful Christ follower at the ripe age of ninety-seven, but rather, I am being asked to prayerfully take the next step with awareness that God is with me. If I do that, the journey will be much more fulfilling and enjoyable. Excuse me. I think I need to get my shoes on first. Then comes the next step.

July

Be Attentive

This weekend, I barely avoided a wreck because some distracted driver was texting as they left the parking lot. They never looked up, although my truck, with its screeching tires, should have been pretty obvious. I stopped and allowed her to continue unabated. The last I saw her, she was still texting as she drove down the highway. I prayed for the people she would be meeting. That is not unusual in today's culture. It may have happened to you. Because of the pace of our society, there are many distractions in our effort to keep up. Cell phones regularly interrupt important conversations, even prayers or spiritual services. I have been guilty of saying, "Uh-huh," later realizing I cannot remember what was being said. I was too distracted.

I think distractions leave me like the two people traveling to Emmaus (Luke 24), who walked with Jesus but did not recognize him until they sat at the table of hospitality together. It took sharing space and a focused ancient process to realize that they were hosting the very one they had been mourning. I wonder how many times I have been so distracted in my life that I miss the presence of Christ. Like the travelers, I need to be attentive to my "burning heart" (Luke 24:32). My motto tonight: "Eldon, be attentive!"

Big Sky Country

I USED TO SLEEP UNDER THE STARS IN IDAHO. MY BROTHER AND I would move our beds into the backyard. We loved sleeping under the tent of stars that some nights would be framed by the brilliance of the northern lights expanding to the Milky Way. Our little house was hot, but outside we would catch the cool evening breezes and need to snuggle under the covers. We had no need for an alarm clock because our crazy rooster would crow at the first hint of sunrise, which would cause the mule to bray. It was the most effective alarm clock I have experienced (Idaho is truly different.)

Recently, I read a text that reminded me of the wonder I felt lying in bed and observing the stars and attempting to name constellations (Psalm 19). "The heavens proclaim the glory of God. The skies display his craftsmanship. Day after day they continue to speak; night after night they make him known. They speak without a sound or word." The majestic silence of Big Sky country, where the air is easy to breathe and it seems as if the horizons, which are stretched to capacity, "proclaim the glory of God." Yet, as the shepherd psalmist understood from the night watches in Israel, "they speak without a sound."

I have reflected on how my life speaks without words. I am certain that neither my words nor my silence always glorifies God. Yet, I have this overwhelming desire for my being to honor the God who crafted this Big Sky country. Tonight, I am silent, and as darkness surrounds me, I prefer sleeping inside, but deep within, there is a longing to hear the silence of creation and feel the sense of awe and wonder that I felt those nights long ago in Idaho.

Exploration

WHEN I WAS A CHILD GROWING UP IN IDAHO, MY IMAGINATION was ignited by thoughts of Lewis and Clark's great adventure through the area where I grew up. I spent days as a child exploring in my grandfather's pasture. Later, in my teen years, I would ride my motorcycle over the back trails in the mountains and explore sights seen by very few. I experienced high adventure when I found a hidden cave or rode into the middle of a herd of elk.

As I reflect on my own spiritual journey, I wonder where the spirit of exploration seeped out. At some point, safety seemed to take priority over discovery. The spirit of adventure was replaced by the desire to settle into the known and no longer push the limits of the unknown or undiscovered.

Tonight, as I reflect on my day and some of the conversations I have had recently, I am convinced that one of the underexplored areas of my life and others is the interior of our being. I realize that my reluctance to explore further means I have missed important discoveries. Jesus gently reminds me, "Seek and you will find" (Matthew 7:7). His very presence within me makes it a worthy place to explore (1 Corinthians 3:16). Maybe I will put on my explorer's hat and venture into the surprises found in His residence.

Maybe ...

Grass Is Greener

A COUPLE DOZEN GOATS AND LLAMAS FENCED IN A FIELD WITH enough grass and weeds to last for several weeks. But this morning, one enterprising llama had its head stuck through the narrow openings in the woven sheep wire fence, attempting to reach the dried-up grass along the roadside. The grass is extra short from a recent mowing by the landowner. As the llama strained, risking being entangled in the now-stretched fence, I laughed out loud and smiled all the way to my office.

That llama is so much like me. It is a bit demeaning. God's generous provision is never quite satisfactory in my eyes. I long for the tidbits just over the fences in my life. I attempt to satisfy my cravings by risking to reach the scarcity on the other side of the fence. Why is it so inviting to me? Like the llama, I do not have blinders; nor is my eyesight less than 20/20. What hidden impulse urges me to stretch my neck where it does not belong? Since it has happened more than occasionally, there must be some helpful pattern to provide insight. The Bible says, "Godliness with contentment is great gain" (1 Timothy 6:6) and admonishes, "Be content with what you have" (Hebrews 13:5). But somehow, that grass on the other side looks so irresistible.

Monastery

WHAT DO YOU HEAR IN A MONASTERY? MONASTERIES ARE made as places to listen. We often choose them as places to hear God. It seems odd that we need to build monasteries when God has created monasteries in nature. But humanity has always seemed to need to create a specific sacred place to be near God. I spent today in a monastery that is sacred because of the dedication to learning and listening that has occurred here. If you listen, you may hear sounds like the muffled work of custodial help or even the banging of pans occasionally emanating from the kitchen. Ancient plumbing contributes its unique moans of old pipes announcing their weariness. Through my slightly opened window, I can hear birds sing and bugs hum. Every once in a while, there is a burst of spring breeze cooling us with its icy edge. I can hear whispered voices and eerie whistles of the trains, but there is a specific sound I deeply desire to hear. It is the voice of God.

While this place has a special place in my heart, it is not a given that I or anyone else will hear the voice of God here. But it is a place where my heart can grow silent, and that raises the chance that I might hear more clearly than in the noise I surround myself with daily. Monasteries remind me to remove myself from the hideaways of my life and become open to God and the truth. Noise in my life often replaces or prevents truth. Silence creates a moment where truth can be heard. It takes courage to hear it and embrace it. So, tonight, I am listening, and I pray for courage to hear the truth.

Old Friends

TODAY, I RECEIVED A CALL FROM SOMEONE WHOM I HAVE NOT talked to on the phone for almost thirty years. He called "just to speak blessing over my life." He is that type of friend. We have walked through challenging times together that forged a bond that exists, no matter how long between communication opportunities. Our conversation was primarily about our spiritual journeys and our commitment to continue to grow into what God desires us to be rather than a game of one-upmanship about who has achieved what recognition.

I have a sense of joy as I reflect on the joys and challenges we experienced together in ministry. I realize that in this season of our lives, we carry the mantles given us by society loosely and find ourselves focusing on the inner workings of our souls. Both of us have faced death, but we have survived, and somehow, we have a sense that there remains work for God to accomplish in us and through us. We spoke of the fun of our adventures and laughed with each other. Thank you, God, for bringing good people into my life that have caused me to grow as a person. I resonate with Paul: "I thank God upon every remembrance of you" (Philippians 1:3). Old friends are a gift from God.

August

Dark Nights

It is nightfall, and the late-summer darkness is shortening the days of summer. Darkness is creeping toward long winter nights already. There is another darkness that creeps subtly into our lives, but we prefer not to mention it. St. John of the Cross and other ancient Christians were more open to discuss this dark night.

I meet with people in spiritual direction who are struggling with this insidious darkness. Its arrival is often a surprise. It seems to be avoided in proper Christian circles. Yet, the dark night, as mysterious as it seems, is much more common than one might suppose. The dark night seems to bring with it an overwhelming silence, often at seemingly very inconvenient times. The dark night carries a deep desire to hear and know God in the midst of the silence. The desire to listen is why ancients, including Christ Himself, treasured silence. It can become a gateway for growth and understanding.

Tonight, I sit at my desk and watch dusk turning into darkness, and I shiver in my soul, knowing there are people I will meet in the days ahead who will share their concern over the darkness they are experiencing in their souls. But I find comfort knowing that like the seasonal changes dark nights are not forever. My hope rests in the Creator, and I pray for dawn.

Garden

It is empty. Nothing. Like many Pennsylvanians, I built a raised garden this spring. It involved a few hours of work after visiting our local Home Depot. Mountain soil is not always fertile, so I even purchased some enriched soil to fill the small space by our circle drive. However, I did not purchase seedlings. I became distracted by the busyness of the season, so the garden space has remained unplanted. Summer is ending, and I see the farmer stands selling vegetables, friends offering to share their bounty, but I have nothing but good intentions. The garden is empty.

Sometimes, life seems to be one season of planning after another filled with a lot of empty spaces, in which tasks so carefully planned were never completed. The result is an empty garden. While I have many excuses, the fact remains that I never took time to go to the local garden supply to purchase seedlings or to plant them. The result is zero. I can take some comfort in the fact that the neighborhood deer, the fat marmot, or even the rascally squirrels did not feast on my hard work, but neither did my neighbors or I. My garden space lies empty. Dreams fulfilled require action attached to planning.

The Snakeskin

She shrieked as she recognized the creepy skin left behind by a snake. The snakeskin protruded from under the garden hose case. My wife had used that hose recently, and it is located by the step off of our porch. Neither my wife nor I have ever called a snake our friend. We both grew up where dangerous snakes were to be feared. As a result, being surprised by a snake has never been my idea of fun. The legend is that the builders of our cabin in the woods encountered eastern rattlers as they built the house and worked on the acreage. Both carried guns. The snakes seemed to be gone until this skin (not a rattler) showed up.

Snakes simply need to shed old skin from time to time. So do people. I carry baggage that blinds me to my surroundings, much as the loosened skin blinds a snake. While the human process may be very different from that a snake, there is a definite process to shed the skin of my life that I thought defined myself. Throughout Church history, dedicated people have searched for keys to the process of shedding a false identity and release from sins. I just hope we don't leave scary stuff behind.

Traveling

I am a weary traveler tonight. The miles were many, and the hours seemed extra-long even though I enjoy traveling. There was time for silence, prayer, and my favorite CD of music, but I still feel like I am on the road. It seemed as if every truck was attempting to deliver priority materials somewhere. I found myself dodging trucks and avoiding grumpy people zooming around slow-moving sixteen-wheelers laboring up the hillsides. Even the exits were clogged with the smell of diesel as trucks waited to get back into the race.

I often refer to my spiritual life as a journey. The psalmist refers to "walking through the valley of the shadow of death" (Psalm 23). Sometimes today, that shadow of death seemed closer than I wanted, but I arrived home safely, having survived the struggle of the highway.

Hebrews 11, verses 13 and 14, indicates that we are travelers through a land that is not our home. It uses words like "aliens and strangers" and indicates that as people of faith, we "are looking for another country." My home is in that other country. I anticipate arriving safely home and experiencing the welcome to the place prepared for me. My deep spiritual desire is that I find my way home. Right now, I am traveling, but I anticipate the welcome home, so I continue to travel.

Unexpected Gifts

Unexpected gifts are exciting but also humbling. Today was a day of gifts. I received several types of unexpected gifts, such as affirmation from a student, another appreciation from colleagues, another an invitation to participate as educator (an earlier disappointment), another an opportunity to share lunch with a respected leader, and the list went on and on. At one point, someone asked me if they should sing "Happy Birthday" because they were aware of some of the gifts.

Such days are mysterious as unexpected gifts are received, but the thought that others would be willing share time and other gifts with me is humbling. However, gifts are also fun! As I reflect this surprising day, I can only imagine what God, the Author of "all good gifts," must feel as we excitedly open the mysteries of His gifts to us. But I also wonder about God's reaction to the gifts I offer Him. While it is not my place to project my feelings onto God, God has described the joy over the gift of a child returning home. God also finds joy in the offerings we bring to the altar or share with others, but I wonder if God ever thinks the gifts we bring are just fun. Does God grin from ear to holy ear as we bring gifts? (No sacrilege is meant by this.) Is it fun for God to give us gifts? I carefully consider my responses. My response probably reflects who I am more than who God is. Can you imagine God grinning at my questions and my response? That may say something about you.

Wind Blowing

IT IS EXHILARATING TO FEEL THE WIND BLOWING IN MY HAIR and gently tugging against my T-shirt, and all the time, I am wondering if I forgot how to do this. I just purchased a bicycle from my son. It is by far the nicest bike I have ever owned. Will it be a mass of metal if I crash? Will I regret trying once again to do something I have not done for years/ages? Then I am on level ground and just ride along, avoiding cars and refusing to wave at people in their yards because I need both hands to guide my bike to where I am going.

There is much in life that is exhilarating and filled with excitement, but fear and risk demand my full attention. In this season of transition, I find myself wobbling through decisions and struggling with whether I should even consider the challenge to experience the joy of living fully. But somewhere deep within, there is a voice of encouragement that says, "Try it!" Is that the voice of God, or is it the silliness of trying to prove I am sixty years younger? Truthfully, if Christ came that we might have life and that more abundantly (John 10:10), why would I be reluctant to get on the bike of life and experience the wind of the spirit blowing through the spiritual clothing I am wearing? I spent the day with people who are an encouragement to engage the opportunities to ride again. My spirit longs to feel the wind again and see the beauty of life as I ride. Tonight, I thank God for the voices that have joined with God to say that it is important that my faith be active, not passive. The bike waits but not for long!

September

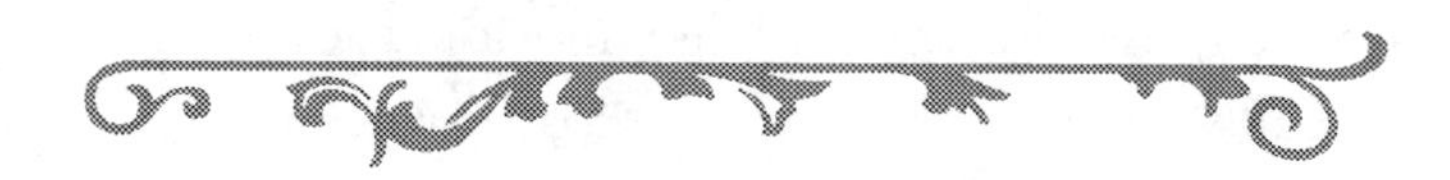

Autumn Arrives

The summer breeze has begun to tease me by lazily drifting by carrying a hidden promise of fall foliage and crispness that says frost will visit. The sun has begun to droop from its summer solstice and finds rest early in the west. Recently, I sat on our porch, enjoying the cool morning and the taste of freshly brewed coffee when I realized I was not alone. The silence was broken by the buzz bombing of hummingbirds arguing over who owned the nectar in feeders and flowers. Beautiful little energized birds were gathering the stamina they would need for the long flight soon taken.

I anticipate the return of autumn, but the changing seasons remind me that time passes quickly. Mothers are posting photos of children returning to school and marveling at their aging. Last-minute vacations seem to dominate social media. Time passes, and somehow, although we all share the same amount of time each day, days seem to be running in my life rather than the snail's pace I felt as a child. "Making the most of every opportunity" (Ephesians 5:16) tends to leave me breathless. My "bucket list" remains a stark reminder of what is left undone. Yet, the passing season also reminds me to take time to listen to the hummingbirds and enjoy the coffee.

Burnable

As a favor, I picked up some trash for burning. As I loaded the pieces of burnables, I was reminded that all these items were once valuable. But now, they are viewed as expendable. Maybe they are only fit to create a bonfire on a cool spring evening. (Right now, it is nine degrees outside, and even the deer are too cold to gather around a bonfire.) I recalled that in my life, there have been some important items I felt I "must have." In time, they have taken their place with other expendable items and ended up in a scrapheap of leftovers. I suppose the lesson might be that I should lower my level of wants and needs or at least be more selective. But today, my imagination ran wild about how these scraps could be recycled and incorporated into a "scrap decor."

Tonight, I am grateful that Christ is willing to recycle the scraps of my life and create value out of my leftovers. I am also grateful for the lesson of years that seems to place less value on stuff. But I also realize that I may need to let go of my stuff and just warm my hands around the bonfire of my former valuables.

Cool Breeze

YESTERDAY, THERE WAS AUTUMN IN THE AIR AIDED BY A COOL breeze that lowered the temperature well below normal. It sent me scrambling for that sweatshirt that I had not packed with winter clothing, but it also reminded me again of changing seasons and how much I enjoy the four seasons. I must admit: fall is my favorite. However, now our cabin sits under a canopy of leaves that fall and need attention.

Life has been changing for me. I realize that I am in autumn, but it is my favorite season because hues of varied colors make for beautiful patterns. That is true in my journey. This season is bringing a variety of opportunities and challenges that mix colors in ways I never saw them previously. At the end of the day, it is exciting to engage each day. I am in awe of the handiwork of God in the midst of my dilemmas.

Tonight, some painful experiences have colored my life recently, but at the same time, new mixtures of hues and strokes fill the brush of life with strokes of gratefulness. When I stand back and gaze, like the multicolored hillsides of Pennsylvania, my life is filled with a variegated canvas reflecting the autumn of life. As I pause, I give thanks to God and pray that somehow God's work in my life reflects the beauty of God's creation like the painted hillsides around me.

Leaves

One of the disadvantages of living among oak trees is that autumn leaves do fall. I wish they were a bit more selective about where they land. Would it be a problem for them to fall among the trees instead of my tiny lawn? As I removed them again today, I noted that some were beautiful; others seemed almost frozen in place and were difficult to dislodge. But tonight, I can rest because for a few minutes, the lawn is once again green. But the next windy day, the few leaves left on the trees and those that blow in from the neighbors will once again cover the lawn in autumn colors.

Life sometimes seems as arbitrary as the falling leaves. Their journey may be whimsical, but sometimes, it seems like they plot against me. The truth is that I do not control leaves or wind or even the seasons of life. When I realize that truth, my frustration lessens, and I can step back and enjoy the beauty of the season. Life is beautiful, and the leaves, like each of us, carry a unique beauty that is a gift to God's world. Too often, that beauty is overlooked. Today, I found myself pausing to enjoy the beauty of those leaves. I need to pause and enjoy the beauty more often.

Memories

THE SOUND OF MACHINERY SHUTTING DOWN ON SATURDAY evening, and the smoke rising from leaves burning stirs memories from decades past. In Idaho, it was common for machinery to stop at sundown on Saturday, and a week's worth of our neighbor's leaves piled high would smolder until only ashes remained. For my grandparents and my nuclear family, Saturday night was a preparation for Sunday. Food was prepared, showers were taken, animals fed and cared for, and darkness turned to silent anticipation of Sunday's arrival.

Today, I watched a movie focusing on Jewish immigrants from Russia and enjoyed their preparation and celebration of Sabbath at sundown Friday. The age-old ceremony portrayed a beautiful anticipation of the Queen Sabbath coming to live among these people making their way in a new land.

It is Saturday evening, and somehow, the memories from Idaho, the Jewish ceremonial welcome of Sabbath, and the neighbors closing down after work today all meld into an expectation that God is among us and celebration can begin. The heightened anticipation and the preparation for realization all work to increase awareness of Immanuel, God, with us (Matthew 1:23).

Tonight, I find worship and celebration mixing with memories to create a deep desire for Sunday and the community that will gather to celebrate God with us even in new places.

Prayer as Desire

SOMEONE SAID PRAYER IS DESIRE. HAVE YOU AWAKENED WITH such desire in your heart for God to move that words are not enough? At such times, it seems like if I do pray, I will need the Spirit to express the words for me because words seem inadequate. I am speechless. I believe that God understands my desire and is actively present and at work in my life through the gate of my desire. The psalmist says that God provides the desires of our heart (Psalm 37:4).

Today was such a day. The heaviness of my heart called out to God with silent pleas void of words. Somehow, God heard the desperation. Surely, the Spirit must have communicated at a level impossible for me. In a matter of hours, God responded with significant yet unexpected answers. It was not my faith that produced these "miracles" because my faith was weak. I simply walked in God's grace today. God carried me even though I did not understand exactly what was occurring.

Tonight, I rejoice in the acts of God who left fingerprints on this work. I cannot tell you why or exactly how, but I can say with confidence as an observer shared today, "That is supernatural." It was not by might or power but by God's spirit. This could be a once-in-a-lifetime event, but the memory will linger on in my mind and join the stories that will be retold to illustrate God at work. Still tonight, my soul is so full of God's grace that I am once again silenced and overwhelmed but eternally grateful. It is day that will be remembered.

October

Attentive

I WATCHED WITH AMAZEMENT AS THREE DEER LEISURELY FED on the lawn of a friend. A group of us were meeting in a country home, and I watched in rapt attention. The presence of the deer put me on high alert. I became attentive to my surroundings, such as the way the wind was blowing and observed the busy squirrels so totally focused on gathering walnuts they did not warn the deer of a human presence. (I think that was the Idaho hunter stirring, although I hunt with a camera now, not a gun.)

As I drove away, I realized that it was only a couple of weeks until archery season, then gun-hunting season, began. I imagined deer counting the days until it was no longer safe to be leisure about anything. Amid that reflection, I thought about my own life and how my schedule crowds out good rhythms of simple living. The countdown until the next event raises anxiety and activity so that attentiveness suffers.

I recall Jesus calling his disciples to "consider" things like the lilies of the fields, birds in the air, fig trees, and other parts of their contexts. I miss important life lessons when the demands of life crowd out the attentiveness to my surroundings and how God may be speaking through them. My soul suffers from inattentiveness. I need to stop and "consider" more often. There is so much to be learned along the way.

Celebrate a Life

Life takes surprising turns. A man who was a successful pharmacist found his interactions with customers so meaningful that, like the disciples, he walked away from his livelihood and became a spiritual director. His gentle spirit, life wisdom, and willingness to prayerfully listen to those who came to him endeared his many "spiritual directees," as well as family and friends. This man passed away this week from a battle with Parkinson's, and we mourn our loss but celebrate his life. We admired his willingness to allow Christ to so transform his life that he affected anyone who spent time with him in any context.

Spiritual life can become esoteric and ethereal, or it ends up at the other extreme of legalism, which is focused on making rules for everyone to obey or suffer. But Christ talked of another kingdom, which was neither ethereal nor a matter of keeping rules. He described this kingdom as one that brings life and lives life fully. This life Christ spoke about is one that will touch our total being to provide purpose and meaning. Maybe that sounds like a sermon, but that is not my intent. These comments come after listening to the messages at funerals. There is no review of who drove the sexiest car or lived in the best neighborhood. There is no notice of how well they kept the rules or sharing esoteric highlights. It is always about how people lived meaningful lives and affected others. I believe that, innately, we are drawn to find meaning and purpose. Sometimes, a life path takes twists and turns that are unexpected, but in the end, we will be known by how God at work in us has allowed us to become a person embracing the qualities we ascribe to Christ. It seems like a lifelong process. I have so far to go, but I find comfort tonight knowing I will never be bored.

Darkness

NIGHT IS OBVIOUSLY DARK, BUT THERE ARE MULTIPLE LEVELS of darkness. I recall Idaho nights with spectacular northern lights playing in the sky, but there were nights in which the stars and moon were hidden and darkness seemed to fill all space. It was the kind of darkness that hurried my steps as I stretched for the door to the back porch and the resulting penetrating light. Safe at last.

As I sit here this evening after writing about the dark night of the soul, I realize that like those Idaho nights, there are multiple levels of darkness. The dark night is distinguished from others because it is a time of deep desire to experience God and to receive some sense of direction or answer to prayer. Other darkness may be birthed by a shattering event that leaves a deep ache in our hearts, like the untimely death of my brother. Depression, on the other hand, seems to be darkness where desire is absent and hope is lost. The dark night is marked by a crying out to God but a sense of empty silence.

As I shared with someone today, the dark night is a time in which God trusts us with silence; the key is whether I will trust God in the silence. The words of Proverbs seem appropriate: "Trust in the Lord with all your heart" (3:5). The emptiness of the darkness echoes that reminder. It is about trust.

Fall Foliage

As we drove through the brilliance of the multicolored landscape of Pennsylvania with the sunshine drawing out the hues of beauty, I felt myself immersed in the sensational color lines. Somehow, the Creator Artist provided one amazing view after another that deeply impacted my soul. The blended colors of fall foliage seemed to affirm somewhere deep in myself that my struggling thoughts and decisions could ultimately blend into a life of connected beauty similar to the changing masterpiece outside.

As the miles passed and the seemingly endless landscapes faded into the sodden browns of fields of recently harvested, I found myself celebrating the harvest and knowing that harvest is a necessary for those driving giant combines and groaning trucks loaded with grain. I reflected on the process from planting to harvest that mirrors the rhythms of life. Each stage of development of a crop is vulnerable and requires care. But in the end, when the field turns to stubble, harvest celebrations can occur across our land.

Fall foliage differs from the harvested fields of grain. One is very pragmatic and useful, while the other radiates beauty for no particular reason. Both are valued but in different ways. Some of my thoughts simply were ones of good reflection, but others require a decision. Yet both have great value.

Leaves of Fall

Today, I sat with friends on the porch and watched a tree, still green with life, begin to drop yellow leaves that fluttered to the ground like feathers floating on the vacuum of heat. We were prayerfully noting the spiritual qualities of fall. A reading piqued my imagination as I watched the tree reluctantly drop a leaf every few minutes. I was fascinated by the fluttering path as the leaf floated from its source of life. I found myself acknowledging that there are seasons in my life when my heart has fed the leaves of brokenness and sin.

Like the tree, I know I need to loosen my connection with those leaves clinging to seasons past. It is a past pocked and yellowed by unforgiveness, pride, hate, pettiness filling my tree, my life. One by one, I acknowledge my prayerful desire to release them to the ground, but I fear vulnerability and shame in my bareness. I have become used to the foliage covering my reality. Gently, breezes of the Creator whisper, "Let go." I hesitate and at times argue, but in the end, I drop one and then another and feel the freedom of the holy breeze blowing through my vulnerability without shame. Why did I hesitate for so long?

Listening

Today, I listened as the wind whispered its way through the oak trees that surround our cabin. I was enthralled by the symphonic music nature created. The music in the leaves was punctuated by falling nuts that squirrels scurried to gather for the impending winter. The cacophony of sound and movement was beautiful.

Aging brings awareness that I miss some of the sounds I keenly listened to earlier in my life. There are sounds of nature that I no longer pick up as easily as I did as a youth, but there are times, like this morning, when the wind in the trees creates an unmistakable harmony of sound worthy of hearing. Listening is a gift but also a skill.

I sat in silence with someone today, attempting to hear God in my reality. The silence sharpens my attentiveness and helps me to hear and appreciate the sounds of God moving in my space. The ancient words of Jesus echo in my soul: "My sheep listen to my voice; I know them, and they follow me" (John 10:27). Today, as the wind whistled a tune through the leaves of fall, I could sense a living God trying to get my attention. I am trying to listen. Like Samuel, I whisper, "Speak Lord for your servant is listening" (1 Samuel 3:10).

November

Treasured Gifts

What should I do with gifts? Thoughtful gifts are to be treasured. When someone not only goes out of their way to purchase or make the gift but then gives it with a twinkle in their eyes because they know it is a gift you will appreciate, it becomes special. I am grateful for such gifts in my life as I transition to retirement. Some are simply words of appreciation in a variety of forms. Sometimes, gifts come as acts of collegiality. Those bring smiles when remembered. One person shared a book by Anne Lamott, a favorite author, and wrote meaningful words inside the cover. Then there are the special meals, like the one my wife and I shared last night, highlighted by a waiter who brought our Key lime pie with a candle on it and a congratulatory handshake.

I am grateful for the many daily gifts I have received by staying home today for the first full day such as good conversations, watching playful squirrels, speedy chipmunks, and a variety of birds, including a wild turkey wandering through the yard. The radiant beauty of flowers that have sprung up everywhere in colorful displays. Reconnecting with friends and appreciating the retreat center I can use. It causes me to pause and thank God for the daily gifts that sustain me. When I reflect on the gifts of the day where I have experienced

God, May becomes Thanksgiving Day. No, it is not a national holiday, but it is day celebrated and remembered by me this evening, and it speaks of the gift of days anticipated. Gifts such as these are to be treasured, and they are. Thanks be to God.

Facades

Today, a clerk asked me, "How are you?"

It was a kind gesture, an act of engagement, but not really. She expected me to say, "Fine. How about you?" so she could reply in kind, "Fine too." Truthfully, that conversation was a facade, much like the beautiful new-fallen snow that covers up what is beneath. The truth is that beneath the surface of our conversation, hidden in the recesses of our own privacy, is what our reality is today. It is not "fine" for either of us. We are carrying challenges, burdens, and concerns or possibly joys and even a desire to celebrate.

As I look out my window, the falling snow is turning the landscape into the winter wonderland that we sang about last month. I recently had a conversation with someone who, on the surface, seemed to "have it all" and "had it all together." Beneath the mask of everything beautiful was a pain-filled and guilt-ridden soul. It took great courage for that person to move beyond "fine" to share their pain. Sadly, they were convinced that they were the only person to ever have such a broken soul beneath the mask. Thankfully, I was able to say with honesty, "You are not alone." Like the snow, I hope our facades melt so we can embrace the real beneath.

Scarcity

I HAVE BEEN CHALLENGED RECENTLY BY THE WORD SCARCITY. I have come to believe that scarcity can either cause me to hoard my crumbs or lead me to generosity and hospitality. Years ago, I read a book where the Jesus figure was a poor carpenter who eats with a very poor family, without enough food. Yet, as the Jesus character leaves, the wife and mother slips a jar of jam into his pocket, and he reflects that the poor always seem to be willing to give, even in their scarcity.

Hafez, a noted Persian poet, wrote, "Need brings us together. That makes need sacred." I have viewed the battlefield of scarcity as people grasped for the bits of leftovers for advantage. But I have also watched with amazement as people with deep scarcity took the risk to share with neighbors and even strangers. Need can be holy, but even the holy can be disrespected by a consumer culture competing for scarce resources.

As Thanksgiving nears, my best memories are the sharing that came during years of scarcity because I had parents who modeled gratefulness. Today, a friend on a tight schedule took time to call to say thanks and touch base. Even scarcity of time can be holy.

Brother

Thanksgiving Eve is always a quandary for me. I am grateful for the day and season. I am so fortunate to be a part of a congregation that partnered with community folks to prepare and deliver over seventy meals to people who would not have had a Thanksgiving dinner. I am so fortunate to have friends who planned, organized, and volunteered to accomplish what seemed impossible.

But, today also holds the memory of a brother who died too young. He is my hero. He lived life at a level beyond me. He suffered through multiple wounds in Viet Nam and the ungracious return to the United States. He worked at forging a blended family against incredible odds. He laughed and loved and would literally give the shirt off his back if he thought you needed it. Although he lived hundreds of miles away, being with him was the epitome of too-seldom fun.

An evening news program announced that a wind had shut off electricity in Anacortes and then reported an explosion. Soon, the phone call came. My brother was needlessly killed in that explosion on Thanksgiving Eve. I treasure his memory and miss him daily. Tomorrow, as our family gathers around the traditional Thanksgiving meal, we will honor him and his family in our prayers.

Lonely

I HAVE HAD SEVERAL CONVERSATIONS WITH PEOPLE WHO FELT alone or were experiencing a significant degree of loneliness. God created us with a desire for relationships; God honored that need by relating with us as well as providing other people in our lives. We are not alone in this journey. My first reminder is that God is ever present. I am privileged to interact with God as friend with friend. How can I relate with an eternal God as friend? The thought is overwhelming and humbling, but God, in great mercy, has also provided other people that relate to our lives. I look back over the week and know that I have benefited from the interactions of others—the friend who helped me, the individual who gave their expertise to help me accomplish a goal, the person who took time for a real conversation, the one who walked by and laid his hand on my shoulder, the stranger who volunteered his time, and then the person who invited me to share with my gifts with others. It was helpful to pause and remember that I am not alone at all. We have God and many other relationships. Then, the "frosting on the cake" for me is a family that responds in multiple loving ways. This has been a week of family closeness. Alone never, unless I choose to isolate myself. God, family, and multiple other people are there with me. It is good to stop and reflect on how "un-alone" I really am. Right now, I recall a childhood hymn whose words proclaim, "How can I be lonely?" Great question! I don't think I am.

Refusal

The trees in our little acreage have long ago lost their leaves and stand like silent monuments honoring the cold. But one tree has refused to shed its leaves. Although they turned brown and shriveled months ago, the leaves have simply refused to fall to the ground. They weathered high winds, a record snowfall, and numerous activities that have shaken the tree. They refused to give in to the pressures of their environment and remain as a testimony to their distinctiveness in the forest of sameness.

I smile as I glance out of our sliding glass "doors to nowhere" and see the leafy rebel leaves clinging to the out-of-step tree. Their tenacity challenges me to be more than a lockstep reflection of my culture, living a copycat existence when I have the opportunity to a distinctive lifestyle that says, "It is OK to not fit into the confining boxes of my environment or even the expectations of others." It feels odd to stand defiant in the midst of acquiescence. However, I recall the words of my Savior: "Whoever stands firm to the end will be saved" (Mark 13:13). Difference is not just stubbornness but a purposeful resistance to the influences and rhythms of my surroundings that offers a message of hope to others. Refuse to let go.

December

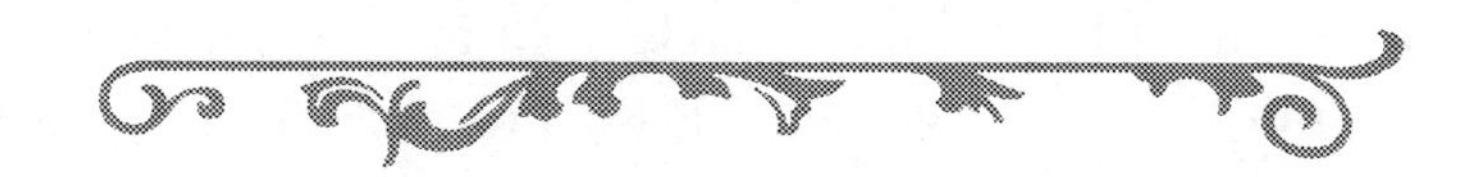

Advent, Day Three

I READ THIS PRAYER TODAY ADAPTED FROM THE BELGIC Confession, "Everlasting God, it's Advent once again. We've eagerly waited for change, but it appears little has happened." Recently, I met with someone who feels like he is in the waiting room of life. Unfortunately, that is a theme common with many of the stories I hear. These are high-energy people with even higher hopes. Yet, the pause as they wait for God to move seems like eternity. Reading the action-packed biblical stories and listening to testimonies about an "all-of-a-sudden" God stirs visions of a God who every day makes something extraordinary happen. This "waiting" God seems unnatural, even unbiblical. Except the Bible is filled with godly people who waited. Sometimes generations passed without the remarkable happening.

But something happens in those who wait. What takes place in me while waiting may be more important than the realization of what I am anticipating. Christmas is the ultimate realization, but so much occurs in the preparation. On the surface, "it appears little has happened," but deep within, in the darkness that is now, a silent God works, preparing my heart for what lies ahead. Advent is a time of stirring and a call to change. However, God's deeper work happens in my waiting place.

Advent

Have you asked, "Where is God in all this mess?" Maybe not you, but I have. An Old Testament prophet, Malachi (3:1–4), directed his message to people asking this very question! In light of the recent catastrophes—such as terroristic acts of violence, death of friends and family members too young, and the person who got our parking place (just kidding; that is low on the catastrophe list, although it can cause some serious anger)—it seems as if an almighty God could lift a finger and halt these crazy scenarios. But for whatever reason, God has not.

A good friend sent me a thoughtful article entitled "Contemplative by Catastrophe," by Parker Palmer. It reminded me that I often need a major shift in my life, often an unpleasant one, to awaken me to reflect on the reality around me. Even in the busyness of pre-Christmas preparation and interaction with friends and colleagues, a seismic shift in my life can cause me to see my illusions and challenge me to enter the doorway into a newly realized reality. Malachi reminds me God has already established justice through His supposed work in me. Where is God in this mess? When I feel God is no longer at work in this world, "it is time to make sure that *ours is* visible to someone."

Squirrels

I HAVE NEVER OBSERVED DETERMINATION LIKE THE stubbornness of the squirrels in our backyard. They have emptied and virtually destroyed bird feeders despite some of my best efforts to discourage them. I finally reconstructed a feeder so that they cannot get into it, no matter how devious their attempts. We also have grandsons with air and pellet guns that have tried to reduce the squirrel population when visiting. But despite the odds, the squirrels still show up with regularity. Right now, we have about eight varieties of birds feeding and a squirrel on the ground below quietly scavenging the crumbs from the feeder.

I wonder at times if the Lord looks at me like I view the squirrels. Is God discouraged by my determination to get what I want despite His efforts to close doors? Do I do damage in my stubborn willfulness to "do it my way"? Do I claim a territory as mine because I see it as a place where I can get what I want even when God sees a healthier source for my life? Does God ever shake His head in dismay at my stubborn willfulness while wondering what motivates me to continue to engage in some of my often-repeated frustrated behaviors? Advent invites me to a new feeder for my soul. The carol encourages, "Let loving hearts enthrone Him."

Lights in the Snow

TODAY, I PUT CHRISTMAS LIGHTS UP ON A TREE IN OUR FRONT lawn and our Bethlehem star over our front door. There was a cold breeze blowing disguised as an icy wind whistling around the corner of our cabin, numbing my hands with cold. I came inside to warm my fingers and thaw out my hands. During that time, at the exact moment one would expect, it began to snow outside. Big, soft flakes began to fall, making the scene in the emerging darkness look like one of those Christmas snow globes. I was captivated by the scene like a child fascinated by the snowflakes in the glass.

I wonder if there were moments in the Advent season when the people of the biblical text paused to note the beauty of their surroundings, or is this phenomena only as we remember the Christmas season? What is it about the expectations of Advent that calls me to pause and soak in the beauty? Muses have questioned that topic through the ages. The answer resides in the carols we sing, such as "Silent night, holy night. All is calm. All is bright." Somehow, in my reflective imagination, this grandeur of creation brings me closer to the Creator. God with us—truly a holy moment!

Sentimental

DO YOU HAVE A FAVORITE SOMETHING THAT IS WORN OUT AND past its prime but holds too many sentimental memories to throw away? It might be a pair of jeans, a pair of shoes, an old shirt or blouse, or an item in your house. I have an old briefcase, worn out long ago from everyday use and worldly travels. People look at me strangely when I show up for an event carrying it. While I admit I am not always into purchasing new things (a result of growing up poor in Idaho), I actually own another new briefcase, but the old briefcase holds more memories.

Tonight, I own my quirkiness. I also realize it is symbolic of other things in my life. Some ways of doing things, other ideas and life patterns, could (and probably should) be tossed. But they hold valued memories, and the familiarity says, "Keep them," even when I know I should let go. As a friend and I caught up on past times, I realized that even in my spiritual life, I hold on to familiar patterns and ways of approaching situations although God calls me to a new, fresh approach or way of processing life. The old ways are comfortable and, like the old briefcase, may be past their effectiveness. They need to be released rather than clutched.

Letting go of past methods was the challenge of the wind of the Spirit blowing in the New Testament. Old ways had been good, but the new had come, and familiarity was not a good reason for holding on. I confess, sometimes, I like to hold on and call it "faithfulness" or "loyalty," when in reality I am just more comfortable with the status quo. Years ago, I read a book (several times) entitled *Dream a New Dream*. A new dream means letting go of the familiar because a new wind is blowing. Even now, I know that I need to embrace the new.

Shadows

THE MOON GLOWED LIKE SOME POWERFUL HAND HAD TURNED a switch onto ultrabright. My usual journey through a darkened kitchen to the life-giving coffee maker did not demand counting steps or touching markers to not trip my way. When I passed the kitchen window that opens to our little forest, the moonbeams bounced off the snow-covered leaves and created shadowy works of art filled with squiggles and shadows crisscrossing each other in the land, anticipating dawn. I paused for some unknown time, simply letting this beautiful landscape soak into my soul. Nothing dared break the silence of the predawn forest. It was simply silent and magnificently beautiful.

I have reflected on the shadowy times of my life that I have usually equated to an ominous fear, and I realize in retrospect that they contain a certain beauty and value that emanates from the Light. As we cross the calendar from Christmas to Epiphany, I resonate with the passage: "The light shines in the darkness, but the darkness has not understood it" (John 1:5 NIV). I feel a little more understanding of the psalmist, who talked of the "valley of the shadow of death." (Psalm 23: 4 NIV God is with us in the shadowy times. In retrospect, the shadows created from God's gift of light shape a work of art.

Concluding Thoughts

This book was written out of an ancient spiritual practice of being attentive to the daily realities of my journey. It is offered as an encouragement for you to write those observations that emanate out of your mindfulness to the witness of nature, people, and events.

Printed in the United States
by Baker & Taylor Publisher Services